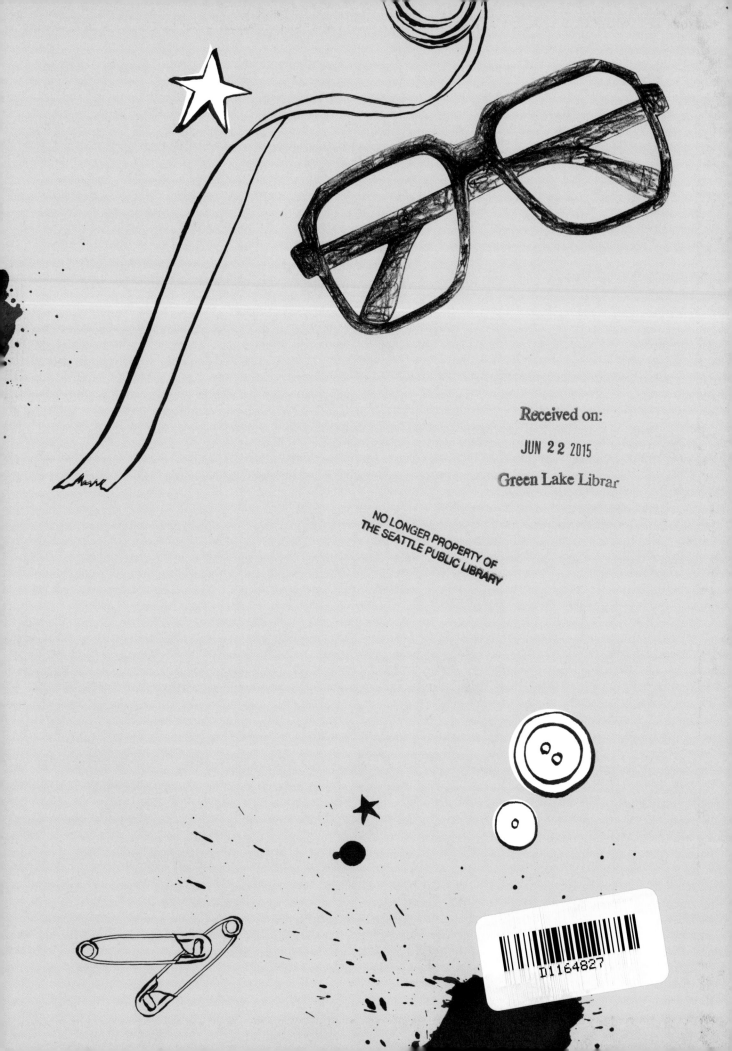

# SEW FAB

## SEWING AND STYLE FOR YOUNG FASHIONISTAS

LESLEY WARE

Laurence King Publishing

Published in 2015 by Laurence King Publishing Ltd
361–373 City Road
London EC1V 1LR
United Kingdom
Tel: + 44 20 7841 6900
Fax: +44 20 7841 6910
e-mail: enquiries@laurenceking.com
www.laurenceking.com

ISBN: 978-1-78067-404-9

Book design by Eleanor Ridsdale
Illustrations by Sabine Pieper

Printed in China

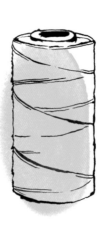

# CONTENTS

**Key**
Look out for these icons as you go.

 Have an adult give you a hand

 Sew by hand

 Use a sewing machine

# CHAPTER 1

# HI STYLE

Fashion is like the wind — it surrounds us, it changes direction, and we love when it keeps us cool. Since fashion is impossible to escape, it's smart to learn all you can.

The first step in this journey is learning to choose the fashion that is best for you. In this chapter you'll discover your Style Tribe, new colors to wear, fashion must-haves, and print mixes to try!

# Fashion, Style, Trends

Fashion, style, and trends are different things, but can be friends.

### Fashion

Fashion is expression and beauty though clothes. If your wardrobe were a language, fashion would be all the words that you adore.

### Style

Style is how you piece together your look with fashion. It's the first thing people see. Style is your own special way of using words, like a song or a poem.

### Trends

Trends are what is now and what is next in fashion. Trends would be the words like "lol" or "OMG" – until everyone else is using them, and they become part of fashion. For example, in the early twentieth century camouflage was only used for soldiers' uniforms. It became a trend in the 1970s, and now "camo" printed pieces are a must-have for many.

— **TIP** —

It's okay when trends and your own style are not friends.

# Look in the Mirror

Take a look in a mirror. What is your favorite thing about your outfit? What makes it fancy or special? What would you change, if anything?

Think about what you love. Maybe you made your earrings, or are wearing a scarf that makes your hair color POP. Style is about individuality. What makes your outfit "you"?

# Find Your Style Tribe

A Style Tribe is your fashion family – a group of fashionistas linked by a common style. Have you ever looked at what someone was wearing and thought "we could be friends"? These are the girls likely to have some of the same pieces in their closet (wardrobe) as you have in yours. Use the shoes to guide you to your fashion family.

What's your Style Tribe? If the Tribes on these pages don't fit, create your own!

## Vintage Chick

You always "pop tags" (spend money on clothes) at your local thrift, vintage, or second-hand store. You mix old and new fashions, but your style shines when you are wearing pieces from the past.

## Comfy Chill

You prefer effortless fashion. You like wearing T-shirts, sweaters, jeans, jogging pants, and uggs or sneakers (trainers). You tend to be practical, but sometimes unpredictable!

## Sophisticated

You have classic style and like wearing signature statement pieces, but you also love the drama of a great graphic sweater or printed skirt. For you, less is more.

## Style Starlet

You wear bright colors, and are always up on the latest trends, and anything to lighten the mood. Fashion makes your heart happy!

## Organic Glam

You're into eco-fashion and read labels to find out where your clothes were made. You also know that organic, soy, and bamboo are not treats for pandas. You ♥ the "green" of fashion.

## Mover and Maker

You like learning about fabrics, clothing construction, and design. Always looking for ways to rescue and repurpose old garments to wear, you dream of sharing your fashion passion with the world.

## Geek Chic

You're quirky, cool, and would rather skip the fussiness of fashion. Your style blends several elements and looks. You have a keen knack for what looks good on you, and you tend to go with that flow.

# Over the Rainbow

**Have you ever heard someone exclaim, "That color looks great on you?" Well, that's likely your color.**

Color is one of the boldest elements of design, making it an easy way to showcase your style. Colors communicate. Experts say that pink and red are thought to be approachable, while dark colors (such as navy and black) are more serious.

In fashion, color can help you create optical illusions. Colors can even make you look taller!

You don't need an expert to find your perfect hue — it can be as simple as having a dress-up party with a few friends and then taking note of which colors look best.

Adding new colors to your wardrobe is fun. Try experimenting with some of the colors opposite.

## Blue-hue

Picture a world where everyone ONLY wore the color blue. Baby blue dresses, blue jeans, royal blue vests (waistcoats), navy blue shoes, and periwinkle tights — all day, all night.

Your best friend, your teacher, your entire family (including your pets), and YOU moving about life wearing blue hues. You'd never know who was who! The sky would lose its gleam, and so would the clouds and ocean. Everything would just be a static buzz.

How would blue affect your mood? If you could only wear blue, how would this impact your fashion options? What would you do to create unexpected style?

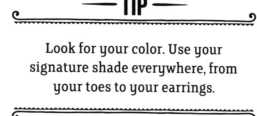

**— TIP —**

Look for your color. Use your signature shade everywhere, from your toes to your earrings.

## Know Your Colors

Your natural beauty is the best asset that you have. Your skin and hair can help you to find the best colors to wear. Look for the skin and hair colors that are most like yours on the chart below. Where they meet are four shades to start with. This chart will help you to not make a mess while mixing (and adding) colors!

— TIP —

Neutral colors do not pop out as much as brights, so they can be paired with almost everything. Black, white, and gray are the most popular neutrals. The different hues of blue, in denim, are neutrals too. For example, black looks good with every color in the rainbow so you can have fun pairing it with bright red or the perfect pink. Create a bold color combo!

**Skin Tone**

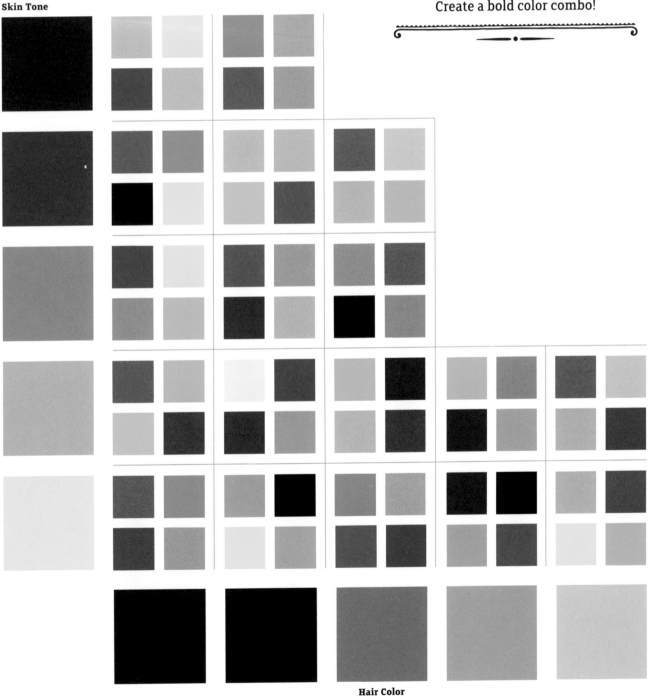

**Hair Color**

# Mix Potions and Pop

So you've found your Style Tribe and figured out your colors – yeah! Now it's time to talk about the mix. It's likely that most of the things in your closet are made from fabrics that have simple prints. Oh how fun it is to blend them up.

The key to wearing prints is matching and blending patterns. This applies to everything from hearts to rainbows to polka dots. So, if you're ready to let your prints mingle, you likely have what you need in your closet to get started. Be a print-cess!

## It's a great idea to select patterns:

★ With similar colors – this lets opposites attract without being too extreme.

★ With different print sizes – "clashing" is chic, but looking jumbled is not. Make sure your mix has enough contrast.

★ With shapes that are complementary, for example a pretty floral with cheetah print or stripes.

## When creating your look, be sure to:

**Pull out your prints**
Shop your own closet before buying or making something new.

**Break it up**
Select a solid (single color) hair accessory and shoes.

**Layer it**
By adding a sweater or jacket, you can wear your outfit to school, and then to an after-school activity.

**Let your personality shine**
Choose clothes that suit your body type, and patterns that you love the most.

# All Mixed Up

Get scrap happy and create a mood board. Use bits of fabric, old fashion magazines, stickers, glitter, and anything else you can find to create your personal style collage.

## What you need

- bits of fabric, yarn, buttons
- fashion magazines (get permission before cutting if they're not yours)
- scissors
- glue stick
- stickers
- glitter
- 11 x 17 inch (28 x 43 cm) piece of paper or cardboard (to stick collage on)

### 1. Gather scraps
Flip through the fashion magazines and find what resonates with you. Look for printed pieces of fabric that can go together. Find wildly odd and creative combinations that you like.

### 2. Cut
Cut out the pieces.

### 3. Glue
Arrange the pieces on paper or card and glue down.

### 4. Embellish
Add other elements to your collage, such as fabric, buttons, stickers, and glitter.

### 5. Get inspired
Place the collage near your closet or dresser (dressing table). Use it to inspire future outfits.

— TIP —

Start a scrapbook with magazine clippings and doodles of accessories you ♥ and plan to buy (or DIY). Take it on your next visit to the mall to window shop for ideas.

# Fab Fashion Must-haves

When trends fade and disappear..."pouf"! Must-haves are the clothes that you can depend on. Keep these items close and ready to wear, and you'll always feel and look awesome. Must-haves are the puzzle pieces to complete a well-balanced wardrobe.

Your must-haves list will change as you grow, but here's a good place to get started. Take your time and make them using the DIY instructions in Chapter 4.

There's no need to fake it – YOU can make it!

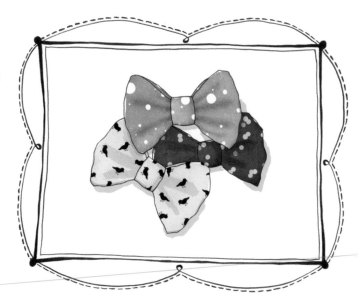

### Unbeatable Bow
Wearing a nice bow, or two, is a trend that never goes out of style. Sew a bow and turn it into a hair accessory.

### After School Tote
You're a girl on the move, so transport your stuff in style. Carrying a reusable tote means you're being good to the environment too. Grab your doll, book, snacks, sunscreen, and glitter – now go!

### Scrappy Scarf
A scarf is the perfect way to complete your look. Scarves can be worn in a variety of ways, including around your neck, in your hair, or on your bag, so there's lots of room to show your style. They can be made from various fabrics, including knit, cotton, or silk. Use your scrappy scarf to update a look while staying cute in the cold.

## Tee-rrific Tee

This is the perfect shirt to go with anything. Pair it with jeans or a skirt, or wear over a dress. It's the best: It's tee-rrific!

## Circle Skirt

The circle skirt got its start in the 1940s, thanks to actress-turned-designer Juli Lynne Charlot. Circle skirts are easy to make. Pair yours with tights, leggings, or skinny jeans. It's cut out like a doughnut – a fun silhouette to wear.

## Little Black Dress

In 1926, Coco Chanel introduced the world to the "little black dress" and now, almost 90 years later, it's a timeless staple in women's wardrobes. Coco wore her little black dress with cuffs and several pearl necklaces. The best thing about a little black dress is you can wear it over and over again – at least until you grow out of it. Make two – one black and another in your color. It's so perfect for an artsy party!

## Loveable Leggings

A classic pair of leggings is a fashion staple that every girl should have. Wear them with a skirt to yoga, or to the next sleepover. Thicker than regular tights, you can jazz leggings up with rhinestones or make them in fun funky prints, such as paisley or polka dot.

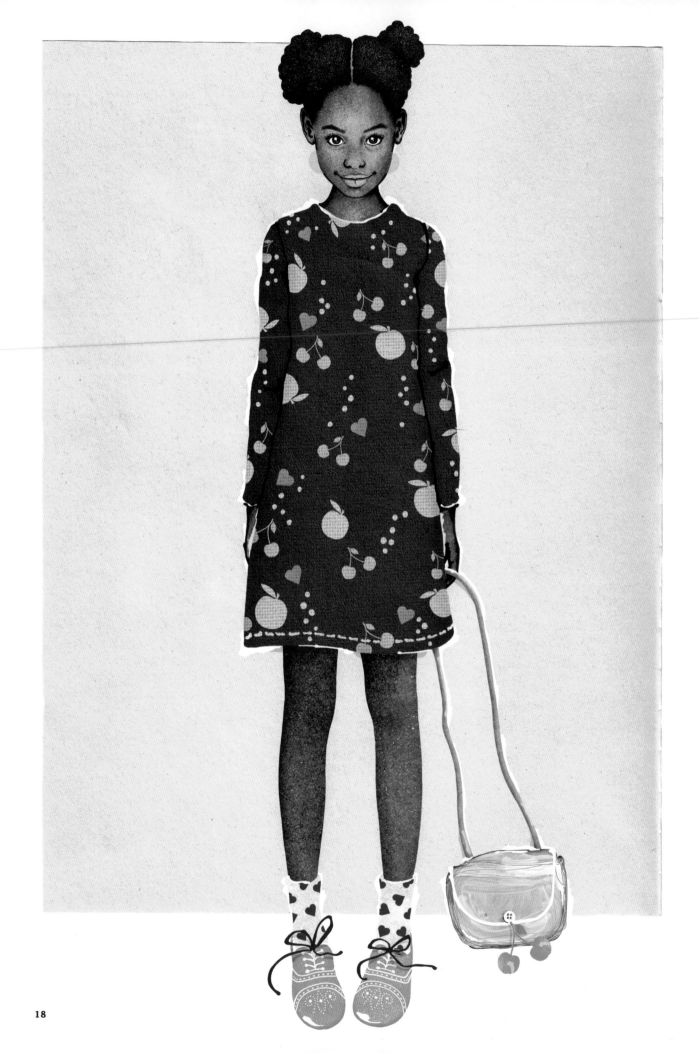

# CHAPTER 2
# LIVE SPARKLY

In the pages that follow, you'll discover how to Live Sparkly from head to toe by expressing your style through accessories that glow. Accessories are like sprinkles on a cupcake. You can pile them on or simply cover yourself with a few; it's entirely up to you!

In general, accessories are either fun or functional. Chunky rings or friendship bracelets are fun accessories. Functional accessories serve a purpose beyond being stylish. For example, a floppy pink sunhat is good for keeping rays at bay but it can also be worn to cover up a wonky hair day. Let's play stylist. Creating fashion is an artful game.

# Super Vision
## The accessory that you'll wear day-in, day-out!

Glasses frames are essentially jewelry for your face. Pick the right pair and not only will you see better, you'll add miles to your style.

### Ready to make your frames work? Consider these tips.

★ Frames are best bought in proportion to the size of your face, but you can always adjust this slightly to fit your style.

★ Frames look best when the topline is in harmony with your eyebrows.

★ Try lots of colors before selecting one. Ask for all the pairs in that style. Fold and hold the frames up to your cheek. Find the hues that are best for you.

★ Consider the shape of your face and your wardrobe before picking a frame. Think balance and sparkle!

### Try these frame styles, based on your face shape:

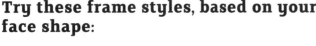

**Face shape:** square
**Glasses style:** round, cat eye, aviator (almost anything will look great on this face shape)

**Face shape:** heart
**Glasses style:** round, rimless, cat eye, rectangular/square, Boston

**Face shape:** oval
**Glasses style:** round, cat eye, Boston, oversized

**Face shape:** round
**Glasses style:** rectangular/ square, oversized

**Face shape:** diamond
**Glasses style:** wire/oval, retro, square, rimless

**Face shape:** rectangle
**Glasses style:** oversized, geometric, conversation starter

# Wish you wore glasses?

Well, you can, even without a prescription. Glasses with faux lenses can seriously frame your view by adding a finishing detail to your overall look.

*Wire/Oval*

*Boston/Preppy*

*Geometric*

*Creative/ Conversation Starter*

*Round*

**RANDOM FACT**

Sunglasses dim the sun's rays while bringing unbeatable brightness to your style profile. Try timeless styles such as aviator and geometric, or far-out shapes like hearts or stars!

*Oversized*

*Rectangular/ Square*

*Cat Eye*

*Aviator*

*Retro*

# Twinkle Toes
## Put your best foot forward

Whether you run, jump, hike, skip, or dance, shoes are considered one of the most important fashion accessories of all. With more than 10,000 shapes and styles to choose from – and a full range of materials, colors, and embellishments – this is your opportunity to step out in style. Think like Cinderella: Look for a perfect fit!

## Toe tips

★ Be sure to stand up while your feet are being measured – feet are larger when the weight of your body is on them. This will ensure that you get the correct size.

★ Select shoes made of canvas, leather, or another breathable material. They'll be more durable and keep your feet from blistering, swelling, or smelling.

★ Shoes can make or break an outfit, so pick them with care.

★ Clip-on earrings add a snap to flats. DIY an instant special-occasion shoe!

★ Red shoes are versatile, which means they go with almost everything. Wear a pair!

# Which three pairs create unbeatable style?

| | | | | |
|---|---|---|---|---|
| **BOOTS** | combat/Doc Marten | snow/ugg | Wellington | cowboy |
| **DRESSY SHOES** | ballerina | Mary Jane | chunky heel | peep-toe |
| **SANDALS** | strappy | platform | espadrille | jelly |
| **CASUAL SHOES** | Converse | basketball boots | loafers | slip-ons |
| **OTHER** | moccasins | slippers | flip flops | Oxfords |

### RANDOM FACT

In the early 1800s, the first Duke of Wellington
requested that his shoemaker change the design
of his boots. The original "Wellingtons" were
made of leather, but in 1852 they were made of
rubber and have been that way since.

# Green Jewels
## The perfect finishing touches

There are oodles of ways to DIY your own bling by treasuring old things. Visit a craft store to get the materials (backs, clasps, cord, etc.) you'll need, and try one of these ideas to create wonderful, wearable pieces.

### Make your own jewelry!

★ Collect unwanted or broken jewelry and rethread it on a colorful cord.

★ Gather buttons and make rings for your ears and fingers by gluing them to a post.

★ Safety pins, paperclips, or hardware look great when connected to washi tape.

★ Make beads from scraps of fabric or old newspapers or magazines. For arm candy!

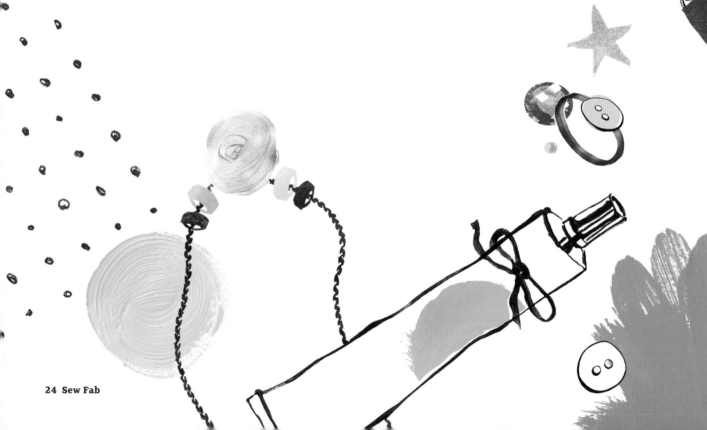

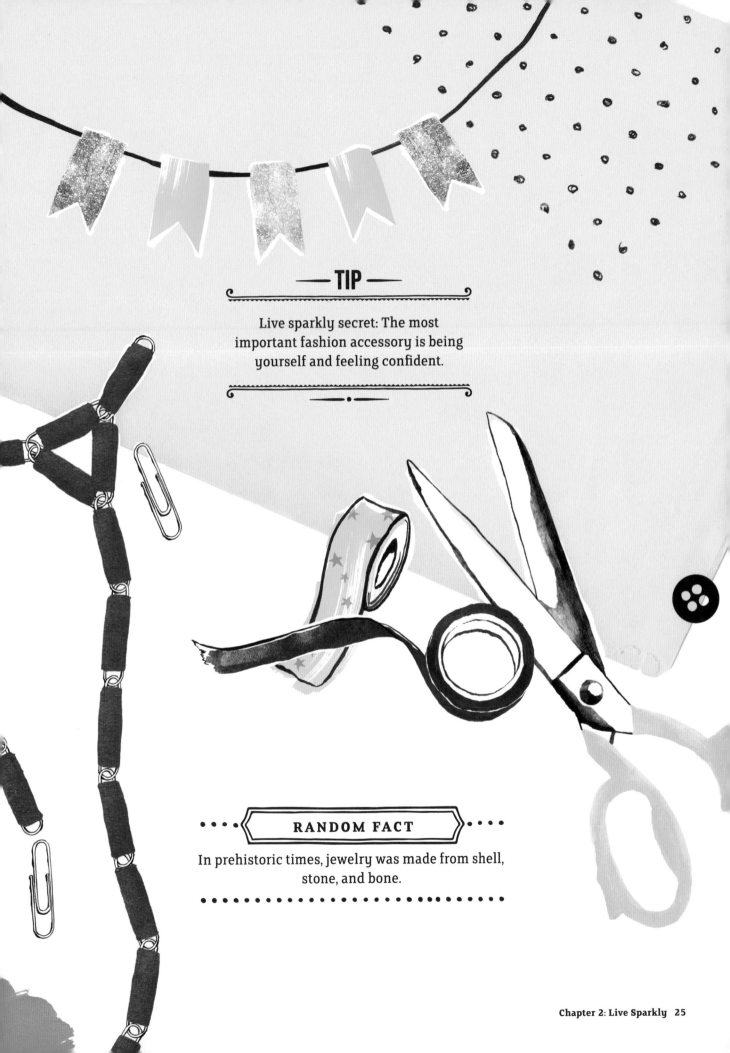

Live sparkly secret: The most important fashion accessory is being yourself and feeling confident.

**RANDOM FACT**

In prehistoric times, jewelry was made from shell, stone, and bone.

# Zap Fashion Drama
## Keep your fashion karma

It happens: Some days you'll go to get dressed and everything just goes wrong. Even the most Zen fashionista will have not-so-fab fashion moments.

### Eight ways to love your style every day

★ Use a full-length mirror.

★ Have a go-to accessory that makes you feel pretty.

★ Respect other girls' style.

★ Limit looking to TV and magazines for what to wear.

★ Stick to your style and always be chic.

★ Surround yourself with quality not clutter.

★ ♥ and care for your accessories and clothes.

★ Forget perfect.

— TIP —

Your smile is an accessory that never goes out of style – it matches everything!

# CHAPTER 3

# SEW READY

You have the sewing bug! From mending your jeans to designing must-have pieces, when you start to sew, your world is altered forever.

Feeling Sew Fab is about having style and being able to sew. After all, the thriftiest way to fashion is to create your own. It's time to design – are you ready to take the leap?

# Get Set to Sew
## What's in your sewing basket?

Sewing requires you to be 100% hands-on.
This means the more you sew, the more skilled
you become.

I bet you are "sew ready" to go, but take the time to learn
a skill that good designers know – how to hand-sew.

## What you need to sew

To truly catch the hang of handmade you'll need to
collect the things on the list below. Some you will have,
some you will need to buy, or DIY.

## Sewing List

**FOR MARKING**
> TAILOR'S CHALK
> COLOR TAPE (see tip on page 47)
> PENCIL
> SHARPIE (marker pen)

**FOR CUTTING**
> FABRIC SCISSORS
> (don't use these on paper, which will blunt them)
> PAPER SCISSORS
> (keep these for cutting pattern pieces)
> SEAM RIPPER (a tool for unpicking stitches)

**FOR MEASURING**
> TAPE MEASURE
> RULER

**FOR PINNING AND SEWING**
> PINS
> HAND-SEWING NEEDLES (also called sharps)
> (packages of needles are usually numbered from 1–12;
> number 1 is the thickest).
> PINCUSHION
> SPOOLS OF THREAD
> POINT TURNER (to help make sharp corners; buy or
> use a chopstick or knitting needle)

**FOR HOLDING SUPPLIES AND IDEAS**
> SEWING BASKET/BOX
> SEWING JOURNAL

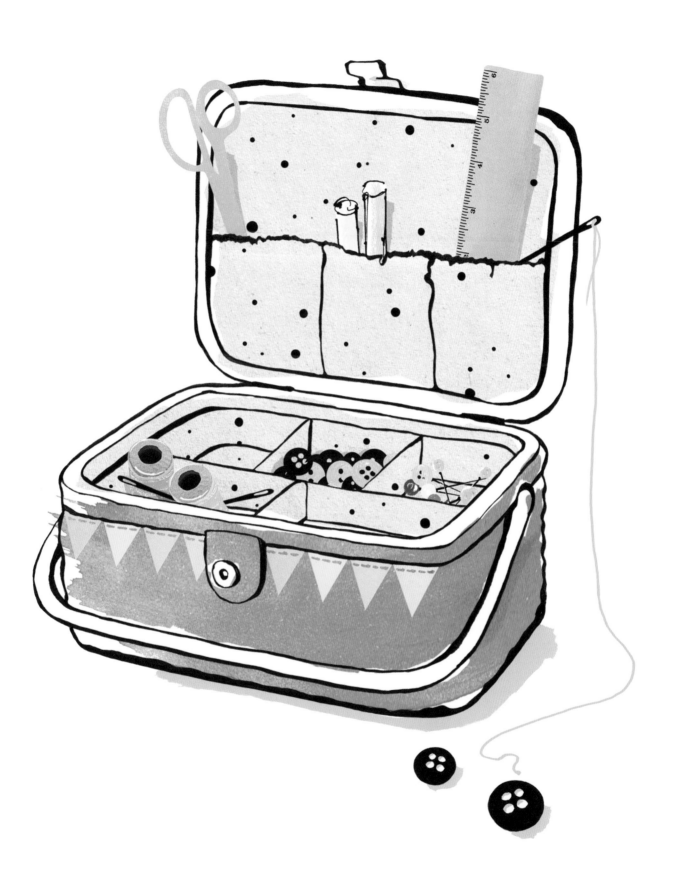

# Mind over Material
**Fabrics are fancy and fun
to collect**

Fabrics come in different weights, colors, styles, and
prints. Revisit Mix Potions and Pop (page 14) for
ways to let your materials mingle.

Your Sew Fab projects all require fabrics that are either
woven or knit. Before heading off to the store to pick up
new materials, read the next page.

Wishing you a fun-filled fabric life!

## Here's the scoop:

### Woven

Fabric in which threads meet at an angle (think of a weaving loom with thousands of tiny threads). Woven fabrics generally have little or no stretch and are lightweight. The most common woven fabric is cotton. Woven materials are easy to work with.

### Knit

Fabric that is constructed with thread that is in loops (think of it as something that you knit or crochet but much finer). Knit fabrics have lots of stretch and are usually a heavier weight than woven materials. Knits can be hard to work with because they sometimes curl during sewing.

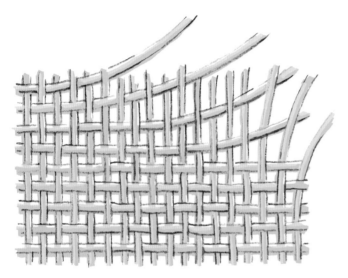

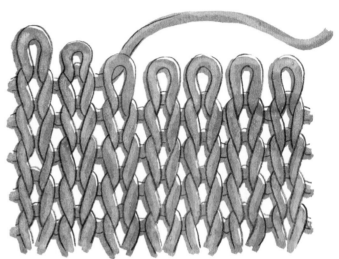

## Which is which?

To tell the difference between the two, go to your closet and gently pull fabrics from top to bottom and side to side and across. If it stretches easily in all directions it's likely a knit. If you can only get stretch across it's likely a woven fabric. Read the label for more hints on the fibers it's made of.

If your sewing project calls for "knits only" it's smart to follow the instruction, otherwise you might end up with a pair of leggings that don't go up past your ankles. Ouch!

### RANDOM FACT

The woven or finished edge of the fabric sometimes has letters, numbers, or dots that show the colors on it. This is called the SELVAGE.

# Creative Space
## Design a mini sewing studio

It's time to start making it – your first sewing studio!
All you need is a corner or closet to transform. Oh,
you'll need a small table, chair, and a lamp, too. Now,
use your imagination to dream up colors, sounds,
smells, and tastes for your space.

### Colors
Decorate your space with a Sew Fab Gallery. Find
vintage fabrics to frame, thrifty pictures, or pieces with
colors, shapes, lines, or textures that inspire you.

### Sounds
Make a playlist. Every studio needs tunes or an upbeat
soundtrack to jam to.

### Smells
Gather good smells. Do you like the tang in tangerine
or something mellow and smooth? Find potpourri, DIY
herb-filled sachets, or adorn with scratch and sniff
stickers. Fragrance and fashion are friends.

### Tastes
Stash healthy treats. Keep granola bars or dried fruit for
your tummy when it needs yummy. With the right fuel,
you'll sew for hours.

## — TIP —

Don't forget a bag or hangers to
tidy your projects when you're
done sewing for the day.

— TIP —

Ask for permission to transform
a corner or closet into your own
sewing space.

# Hand Sewing 101

The pieces in the next chapter would be spoiled by big stitches or crooked seams, so before you learn to cut out and make your own things... let's stitch a bit!

## Let's get going, and start hand-sewing!

1. Cut some thread. Avoid using long pieces because it will twist, tangle, and thin out. The distance from the tip of your index finger to your elbow is a good length.

2. Thread your needle. (The hole in a needle is called the "eye.") Hold it in your right hand (or the other if you are a lefty) and resting on the tip of your second finger. Push the thread through. Twist, or wet, the end of the thread if it's being tricky.

3. Make a knot that is round and small. Ask for help, if needed.

— **TIP** —

It's a good idea to talk through the steps with an adult to make sure you understand how to sew safely. Discuss any sharp tools you'll use. Find out where they stand and where they'll lend a hand.

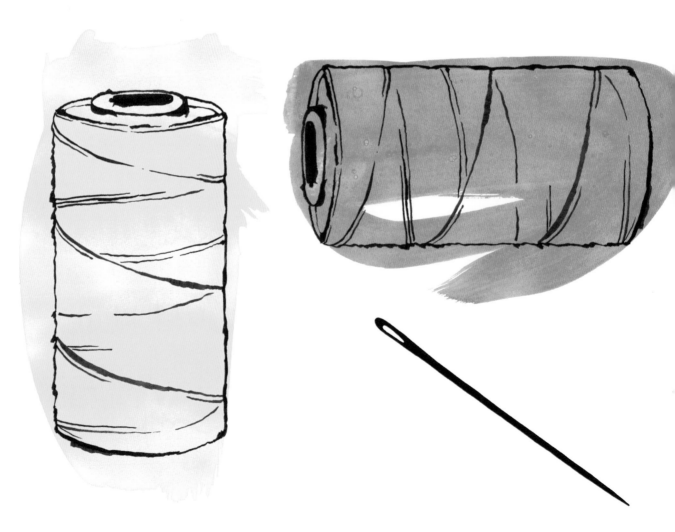

## Now that you're threaded, let's pick up a few stitches.

Practice forming these stitches again and again. Try your best to keep stitches in straight lines, and an even distance apart.

When you finish stitching, or your thread runs out, tie a knot close to the fabric or your stitches will "snap" and "pop."

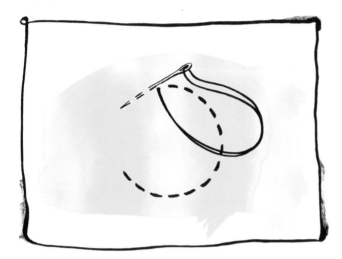

### Running stitch
This stitch is very popular. It's formed by a wave-like movement from the top to the bottom of the fabric and back up. The space between each stitch is even.

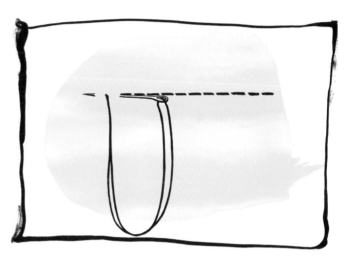

### Back stitch
This stitch is super strong. It's created by inserting the needle in the middle of the stitch before, so that the stitches overlap at half-lengths, forming a line of sewing.

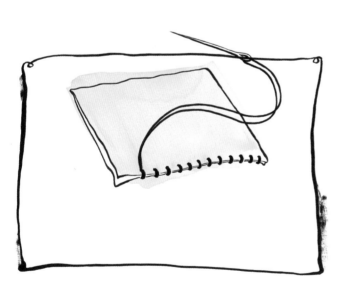

### Whip stitch
This stitch binds two pieces of fabric together using a series of simple loop-the-loops. Whip stitch is useful when finishing projects.

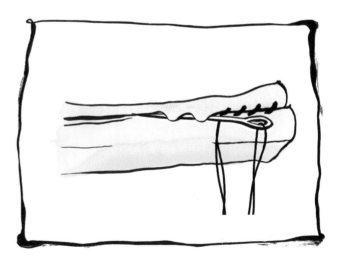

### Invisible stitch
This stitch is commonly used for finishing things and is made by zigzagging the needle in the inner fold of a project. Go to page 38 and try it for your pincushion!

# DIY
# PINCUSHION

Sew an adorable
pincushion! See a
pretty pinning
picture in step 3.

Level

## What you need

- sewing basket (see page 30)
- scraps of fabric
- cotton balls or other stuffing
  (see step 4)

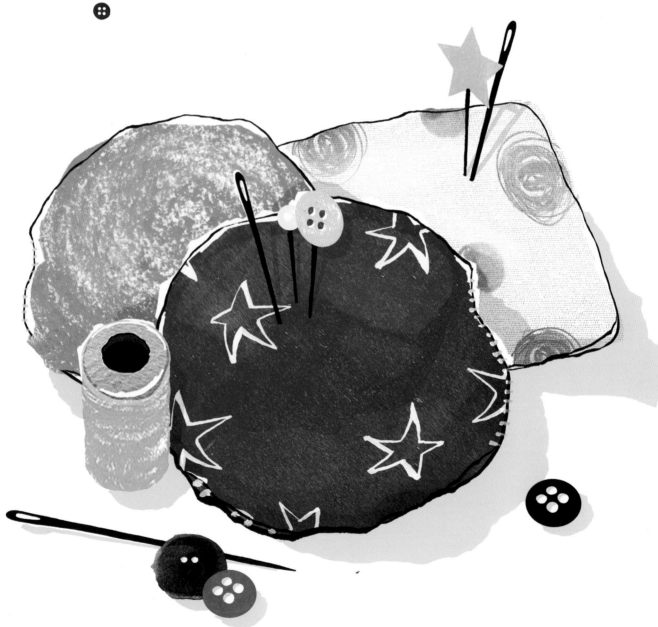

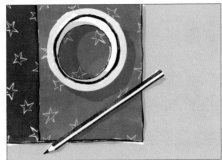

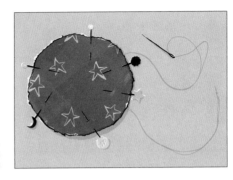

## 1. Gather supplies

Gather your supplies: fabric, cotton balls, thread, pins, a needle, fabric scissors.

## 2. Cut fabric

Make a pattern or trace a shape that you like. Use fabric scissors to cut out two pieces the same size, one for the top and another for the bottom. Place the right sides of the fabric facing each other.

## 3. Pin and stitch

Pin the pieces together. Neatly back stitch around the fabric leaving a small hole. Remember to tie a knot when you finish stitching.

## 4. Stuff

Carefully turn the pincushion inside out. Stuff it tightly with cotton balls, beans, small scraps of fabric, or dryer lint.

## 5. Close

Finish it up by whip stitching (or invisible stitching) to close.

## 6. You're done

Put a pin in it!

— TIP —

Pins keep your fabric from moving when you sew. The more skilled you become, the less you will need to use them. To pin, just push the point down and then up, back into your fabric.

# Dream Machine

You've gathered supplies, started to hand stitch, gained fabric knowledge, and designed your studio. Yay! Now it's time to find the sewing machine of your dreams.

## How to find a machine you'll love and use all the time

Buy the best that you can afford – don't skimp on an inexpensive machine because you will likely end up frustrated. If you don't have lots of money to spend, have an adult help you search for a quality pre-owned machine. You may also want to ask friends and family members who may have a machine tucked away that they are not using.

★ Buy from a specialist sewing machine shop. This will make it easier to return or upgrade if there's a problem.

★ Pick a machine that is easy to use. The fewer unnecessary features and buttons the better. Less is more.

★ Identify an adult who can help you if you get muddled. This could be a family member, or someone at your go-to fabric store.

★ Once you have your new machine, spend time reading the owner's manual. It seems like a bore but it will save you time along the way.

★ Don't forget to name your machine!

**Learn these things before you dive into your projects.
You'll be happy that you did!**

**Getting started**

★ plug in and turn on

★ thread

★ wind the bobbin

★ change the needle

**Sample sewing**

★ operate the hand wheel

★ recognize a good stitch

★ change stitch length

★ reverse stitching

★ control speed

★ sew straight

★ pivot

★ zigzag stitching

# Studio (Sewing) Etiquette
**You're on a roll – yay!**

We're not in charm school, but here's some etiquette to keep in mind while spending creative time.

## Before you sew:

★ Wash your hands.

★ Finish your homework.

★ Have good light – natural light is best.

★ Grab your basket of supplies, keep it close by.

## When sitting to sew:

★ Keep your feet comfortable on the floor.

★ Keep your back against your chair. Don't bend your neck too much. Hold the work up to you, but not too close to the eyes; do not lean over into it.

## When you snip, snip, snip:

★ Open and shut scissors often, keeping the point on the table. Try not to use scissors with worn blades, or your fabric will be jagged.

★ Practice cutting on a striped piece of fabric by following the straight lines. Once you get good, cut circles, hearts, stars, and other bits that you can save and use for appliqué.

★ Hold the point to the floor when moving about. Be careful; never run with scissors.

## After you sew:

★ Neatly fold or hang your work, don't crumple. Wrinkled materials are no fun to work with.

★ Tidy up and unplug anything used.

★ Spend time writing a note or sketching in a sewing notebook or journal.

## — TIP —

Tag your fabric scissors by tying
a scrap to one of the handles. That
way, you won't get mixed up and
use them for something else.

44

# CHAPTER 4

## ART TO WEAR

Let's make art to wear!
Maybe you've been sewing since you were
four, but it's more likely that you're new. With
a few pins, snips, and stitches you'll be on your
way to making something just for you.

The clothing and accessories in this chapter
are easy to cut out and sew. The pictures show
you how to move along, blending your sewing
savvy and style into chic DIY pieces. All you
have to do is follow the directions and play
along the way. It's easy!

# On Your Marks...

## Daydream

Imagine wearing clothes that you've sewn on your own. Maybe you'd like to create a collection of bags and bows that change color in the breeze. Or do you feel inspired to have a ball, and sew a show-stopping dress?

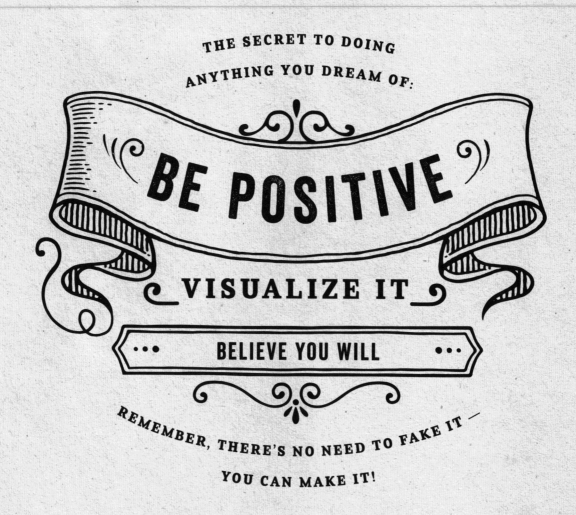

THE SECRET TO DOING ANYTHING YOU DREAM OF:

BE POSITIVE

VISUALIZE IT

BELIEVE YOU WILL

REMEMBER, THERE'S NO NEED TO FAKE IT —

YOU CAN MAKE IT!

# Get Set, Sew

## Follow your "art"...

Practice making these pieces for each season, and they will improve as you grow. At first, follow the project directions exactly. Each time you gradually add your spin. Change the fit, hand stitch a sparkle, or use a special trim.

Before you get set, sew, review the steps with an adult to make sure you understand each one. Find out where they stand, and where they'll lend a hand.

## Let's talk patterns

For most projects you'll need to make the patterns first. Newspaper is the best option for beginners. It already has nice folds, plus it's free!

After you cut out your pieces, make sure you label each pattern with the project's name and include a grainline to ensure you place your pattern on the fabric straight. Grainlines are marked by the long arrow printed on a pattern that corresponds to the lengthwise direction of the fabric. A grainline looks like this:

**Chapter 4: Art to Wear 47**

**— TIP —**

A seam allowance is the distance from your seam to the raw edge of the fabric. All machine-sewing projects in this book have a ⅝ inch (1.5 cm) seam allowance, unless otherwise noted. Use your color tape to make a seam allowance guide on your machine. Keep the raw edge of the fabric lined up with the tape, and you'll sew straight.

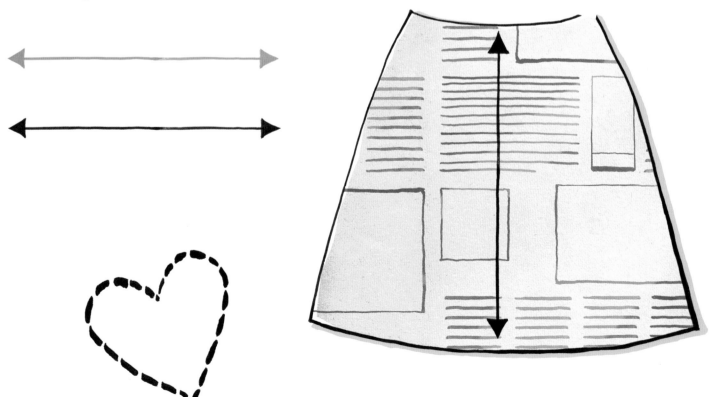

# Dream Machine 101

A. Hand Wheel
B. Free Arm
C. Foot Control
D. Reverse Stitch Lever
E. Extension Table + Accessory Storage
F. Presser Foot
G. Thread Take-up Lever
H. Stitch Selection Dial
I. Thread Tension Dial
J. Needle Plate

K. Bobbin Spindle
L. Bobbin Plate
M. Presser Foot Lift
N. Spool Pin + Stopper
O. Machine Socket
P. Bobbin stop
Q. Thread Guide
R. Seam guide
S. Machine needle

— TIP —

Change your machine's needle once
a month, or every three projects.

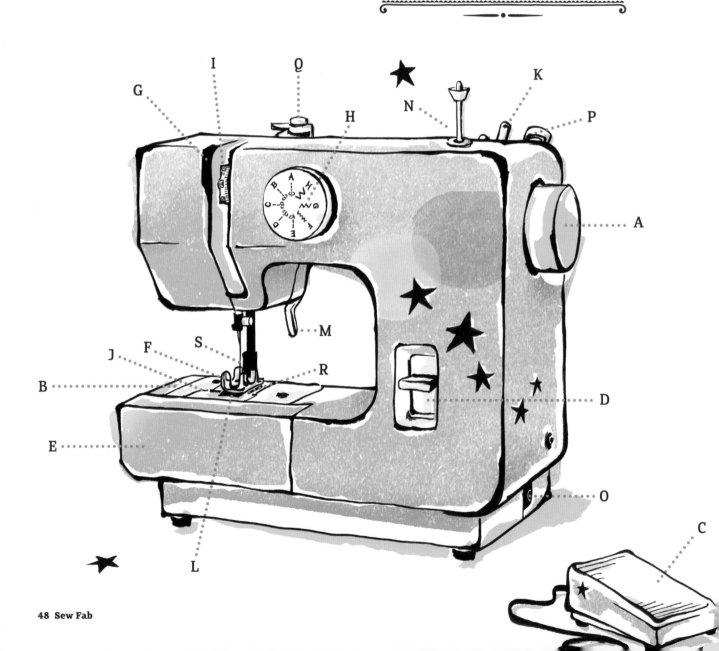

# Need to know when starting to sew

## 1. Starting off

★ Lower the machine's needle (s) in the fabric to be sure you're in the right position. Do this by putting the presser foot lift (m) down and turning the hand wheel (a) toward you. Pull the threads toward the back.

★ Lightly press the foot control (c) and gently guide the fabric along the seam guide (r), letting the machine move the fabric.

★ Note: Never run your machine too fast. Always keep the pressure you put on the foot control steady. The harder you press, the faster the machine runs.

## 2. Reverse stitching

★ A reverse stitch is needed when you start and stop a seam, to lock the stitch.

★ Press the reverse lever (d) and sew for about 1 inch (2.5 cm) in reverse at the start and end of the seam. Be neat.

## 3. Pivoting

★ Stop stitching as you approach the corner of your fabric (use the seam guides on the needle plate (j) to help you measure). Keep the presser foot (f) down and the needle in the fabric.

★ Raise the presser foot and turn the fabric toward you at a 90-degree angle.

★ Lower the presser foot and begin sewing in your new direction.

## 4. Learn more

Review the owner's manual to learn about other stitches, such as zigzag, and accessories for your Dream Machine. Accessories are usually kept inside the extension table (e) and may include extra bobbins, needles, spool holders, and even a brush to keep your machine clean!

In addition to stashing accessories the extension table can be removed to help you stitch sleeves, waistbands, the hem of your pants, or any tube-like parts.

## 5. A bit about bobbins

A bobbin is the small plastic or metal spool that fits neatly under the needle plate. The bobbin thread gets picked up by the thread in the needle and forms the seam line on the bottom of your fabric. The bobbin is important because it allows your machine to form a seam with two threads.

— TIP —

Wind a few bobbins before you start to sew, so you don't have to interrupt the flow by stopping and winding a fresh one in the middle of a project.

# UNBEATABLE
## BOW

Take your tresses up a notch with this easy-to-sew bow.

Level

## What you need

- sewing basket (see page 30)
- scraps of fabric
- hair clip, bobby pin (kirby grip), or headband elastic to attach the bow (you choose)

## 1. Cut fabric

Use your ruler and chalk to draw a 4 x 6 inch (10 x 15 cm) rectangle onto a piece of fabric. Cut it out.

## 2. Pin

Fold fabric in half, widthwise, with the right sides facing each other. Pin.

## 3. Thread

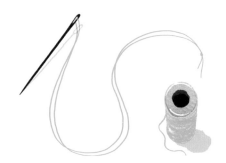

Double thread your needle and knot it.

## 4. Back stitch

Use a tight back stitch to sew around the sides. Leave a small hole – about ¾ inch (2 cm) – on one side. Tie off the thread to secure the stitches, then cut.

## 5. Turn out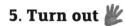

Carefully turn the fabric rectangle inside out. Use your point turner to shape the corners by placing it inside the rectangle, and wiggling it around. Whip stitch or invisible stitch the hole closed. Tie off the thread to secure the stitches, then cut.

## 6. Make bow

Cut a small piece of fabric about 1 x 2 inches (2.5 x 5 cm). Fold the long edges toward the center to make a strip. Wrap it around the center of the rectangle you have just made. Pull tightly and secure by stitching the strip in place on the back of the bow (leave room to slide your hair accessory through).

## 7. Add a clip

Slide your bow onto a hair clip, bobby pin, or a headband. You may need to add a couple stitches or a dab of fabric glue to hold it in place. Bows are the best!

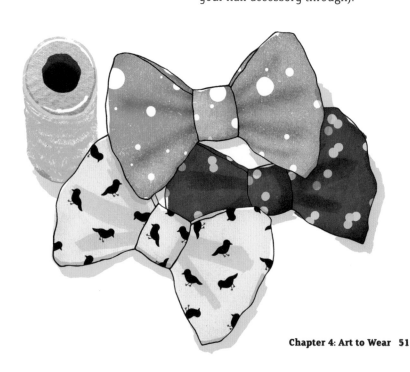

# SCRAPPY

Grab some scraps and
make this super-
simple scarf.

## What you need
- sewing basket (see page 30)
- 2¼ yards (2 meters) of stretch
  jersey or lightweight cotton
  fabric (or scraps from other
  projects)
- newspaper or pattern paper

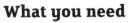

Level

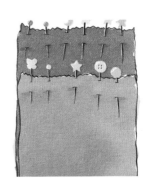

## 1. Make pattern

Make the pattern by cutting a piece of newspaper 26 x 4 inches (66 x 10 cm). The final length of the scarf will be double the pattern length. If you like, change the length or width to create your perfect scarf.

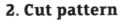

## 2. Cut pattern

Fold your fabric in half and pin the pattern to it. Cut out two pieces at the same time. Repeat. You should have four pieces when you are done.

## 3. Pin fabric

Lay one piece on top of another, with right sides facing. Pin one end and both sides (leaving one end open). Pin the other two pieces together the same way.

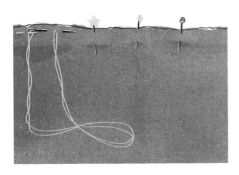

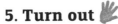

## 4. Sew

Sew along the pinned end and sides of each set, using a tight running stitch or back stitch.

## 5. Turn out

Gently turn each panel inside out (ask an adult for help if needed). For a circle scarf, place the closed end into the open end of each set of panels to create a ring. Fold the raw edge under on each side and sew together with a tight running stitch.

For a regular scarf, sew the open ends of the two pieces together. Fold the raw edge under on one side and use a tight running stitch to close.

## 6. Style your scarf

A circle scarf can be worn around the neck, of course, but you can widen your pattern to create a hood or even wear it across your shoulders like a shrug.

A regular scarf has endless possibilities. Tie it around your neck in a fancy way. Wear it around your waist or even in your hair, if you dare.

— TIP —

When starting a new project, thread several needles so you can keep your rhythm when one runs out.

# AFTER

SCHOOL

# TOTE

**Take the time to sew this tote and then carry it all (on)!**

Level

## What you need

- sewing basket (see page 30)
- ½ yard (45 cm) of cotton for bag
- ½ yard (45 cm) of cotton for lining
- leftover scraps of fabric to make straps or appliqué
- piece of newspaper about 23 x 24 in (59 x 61 cm)
- fabric scissors or pinking shears
- safety pin
- iron and ironing board

## 1. Cut bag pattern

Create your pattern! For the bag: Fold an open sheet of newspaper in half from left to right, and then in half again from top to bottom. Cut a 2 x 2 inch (5 x 5 cm) square along the side of the newspaper that has an unfolded edge (see Tip). Unfold the pattern.

## 2. Cut strap pattern

For the straps: Cut a strip of newspaper 22 x 2 inches (56 x 5 cm).

— TIP —

The little cutout rectangles on each side are called gussets, and will give the bag shape.

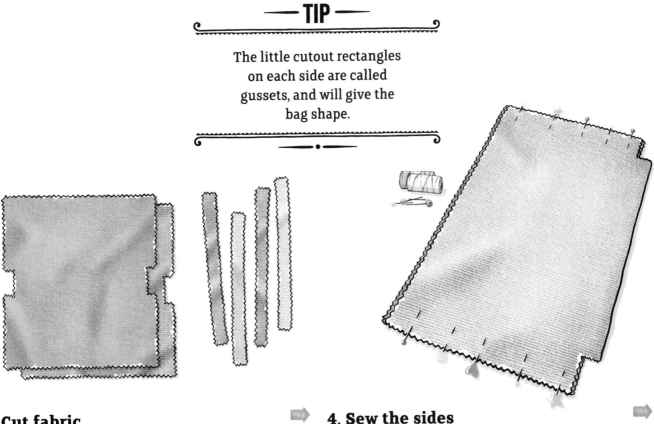

## 3. Cut fabric

Cut your fabric! For the bag: Pin and cut out two pieces using your bag pattern (one for the lining and another for the bag). For the straps: Pin and cut out four identical pieces using the strap pattern.

## 4. Sew the sides

Fold your bag fabric in half, with right sides facing. Pin the two sides. Sew them in place using a very neat hand stitch or sewing machine. Repeat this step with your lining fabric.

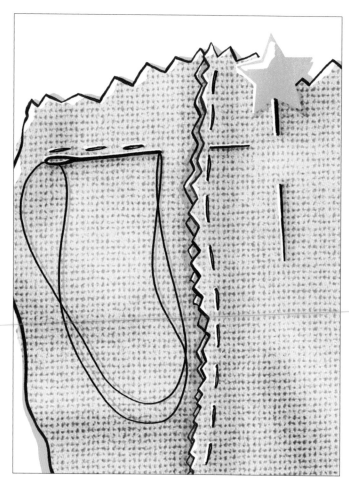

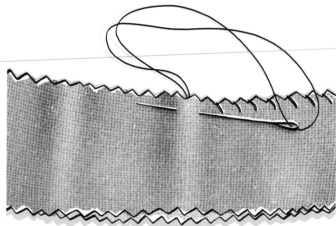

## 5. Sew gussets

Place your pointer finger (index finger) into the open corner of one side of the bag. Pull it closed then pin and sew to finish your gussets. Repeat on the other side and with the lining.

## 6. Sew the straps

Pin two of the strap pieces together, with right sides facing. Neatly sew around the edges and one end, leaving one end open. Repeat with the other two pieces to create a second strap.

Pin the safety pin to the closed end of one strap. Use the pin to help turn the strap inside out, so the right sides are showing. Repeat with the second strap. Press (iron) both straps flat.

## 7. Attach straps

Pin one strap to each side of the lining, so they form a U shape hanging downward on the open side. Make sure that the ends are an equal distance from the side seams. Use a temporary stitch (basting or tacking stitch) to hold the straps in place.

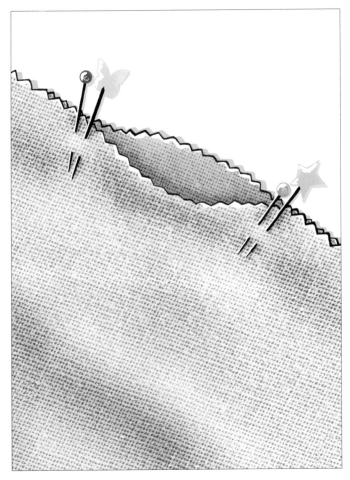

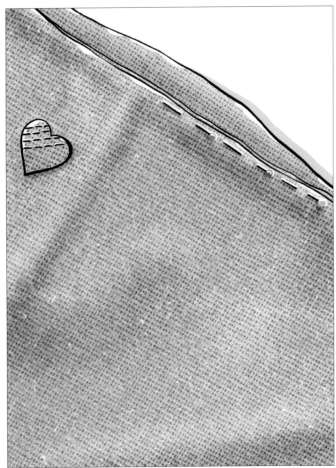

## 8. Add lining

Place the lining inside of the bag with the right sides of the fabric facing. Pin all the way around the outside, wrong side, of the bag and lining. Make sure your straps can **not** be seen at this point.

Use chalk or pins to mark an area on one side — in between the straps — that's about 1½ inches (4 cm) wide. Sew the lining and bag together, leaving the marked section open. This will be used to help turn your bag inside out.

## 9. Finish

Turn the bag inside out by slowly pulling the lining, bag, and straps through the open hole. Once your bag is turned inside out press (iron) it.

If you are sewing by hand, use a whip stitch or invisible stitch to close the hole and secure the straps. If you are sewing by machine, carefully top stitch around the open end of the bag to close the hole and secure your straps.

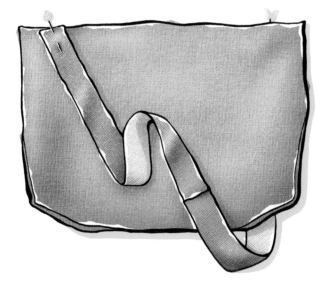

— **TIP** —

When you make this bag again, try using a longer strap to create an over-the-shoulder bag.

# TEE-RRIFIC TEE

Turn up your shine in this trouble-free Tee.

**Level**

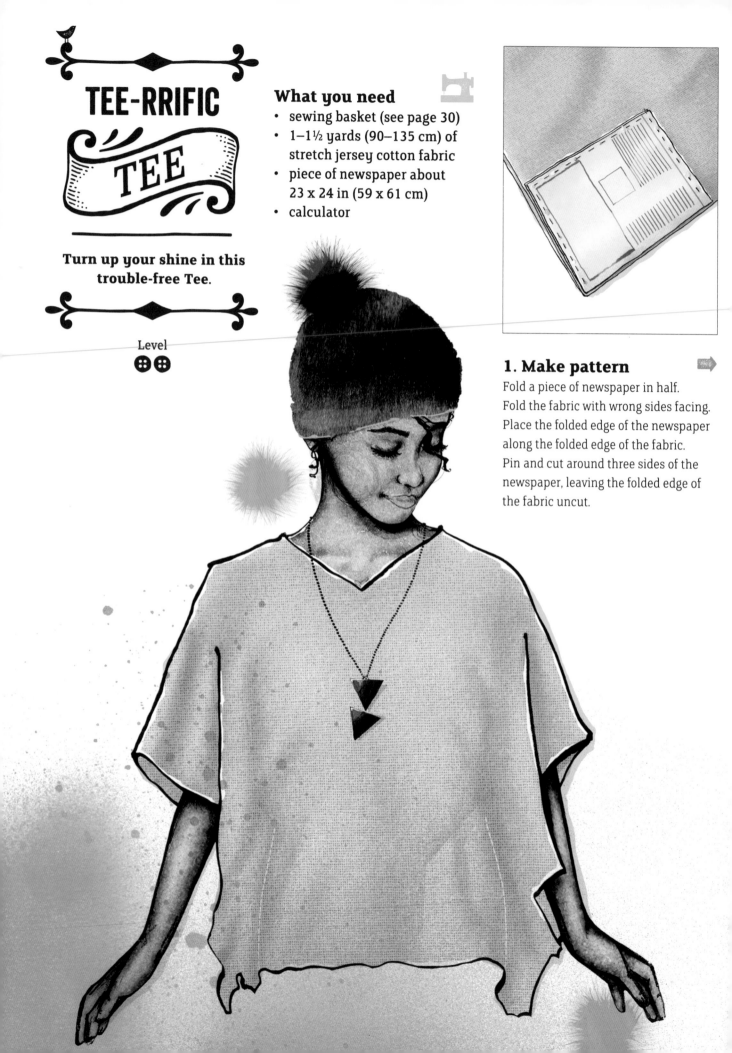

## What you need

- sewing basket (see page 30)
- 1–1½ yards (90–135 cm) of stretch jersey cotton fabric
- piece of newspaper about 23 x 24 in (59 x 61 cm)
- calculator

## 1. Make pattern

Fold a piece of newspaper in half. Fold the fabric with wrong sides facing. Place the folded edge of the newspaper along the folded edge of the fabric. Pin and cut around three sides of the newspaper, leaving the folded edge of the fabric uncut.

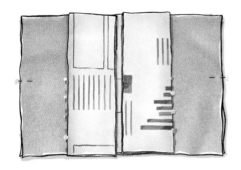

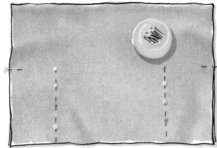

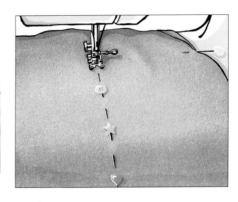

## 2. Measure pattern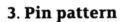

Measure around your bust (chest) in inches and complete this sum:

Bust (chest) measurement [    ] ÷2 = [    ]

+ ⅝ inch (1.5 cm) = [    ]

Turn the fabric around so the folded edge is at the top. Remove the pins from the newspaper. Fold the edges of the newspaper inward, so that its measurement across matches the answer to your sum. Use pins or chalk to mark the new edges as shown. This marks the sides of your T-shirt.

## 3. Pin pattern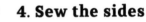

Remove your pattern and measure 6–7 inches (15–18 cm) down from the folded edge of the fabric, for your sleeves. Use a pin to mark the spot. Hold the Tee against yourself to check that there's enough room for your arms to move. Adjust as needed.

## 4. Sew the sides

Sew down each of the sides. Use your reverse stitch button to secure your seams at the top and bottom.

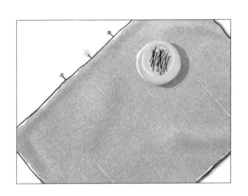

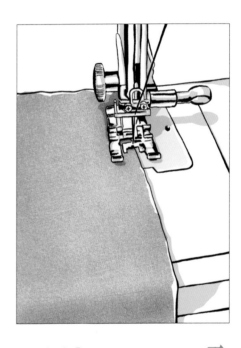

## 5. Create neckline

Use a pin to mark the halfway point along the folded top edge of the fabric. Place additional pins approximately 3 inches (7.5 cm) out from the first pin to create a neckline. Make sure everything is properly centered. Unfold, and cut across, from point to point.

## 6. Shape neck

Decide whether to give your T-shirt a scoop, square, or V-neck. Check your closet for necklines that flatter you.

Use chalk to mark the shape of your neckline, and carefully cut it out. Fold the raw edges under, and neatly sew around to finish.

## 7. Finish

Zigzag around the bottom of the shirt to finish the raw edge if you wish. Or leave it unfinished and rock on!

# CIRCLE

SKIRT

**Cutting just one piece makes this skirt a fun fraction to wear.**

Level

## What you need

- sewing basket (see page 30)
- 1½–2 yards (135–180 cm) of cotton fabric
- 1 yard (90 cm) of 1 inch (2.5 cm)-wide elastic
- calculator
- newspaper or pattern paper
- safety pin

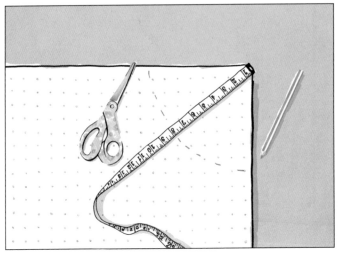

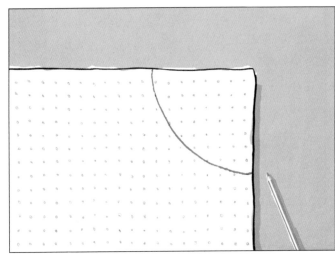

## 1. Draw a curve

Draft your pattern! Measure your waist in inches. Use the number to complete this sum:

$$\boxed{\phantom{XX}} \div 5 = \boxed{\phantom{XX}} + 1 \text{ inch (2.5 cm)} = \boxed{\phantom{XX}}$$

**Waist
measurement**

Open two pieces of newspaper and tape them together to make a very large piece.

Next, use your pencil and a tape measure to mark out a quarter circle in dots across one corner of your paper. Use the answer to your sum as the measurement between the corner of the paper, and the marks that make up your curved line.

## 2. Make pattern

Connect the dots. This is your waistline. Now measure from your waist to your knee in inches. Place that number in the first box and complete this sum:

$$\boxed{\phantom{XX}} + 2 \text{ inches (5 cm)} = \boxed{\phantom{XX}}$$

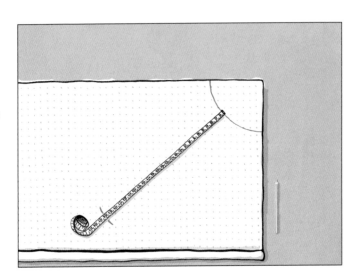

Place the end of your tape measure at the center of the waistline. Create a second curve of dots in the same way you created the first curve, using the answer to the sum as your measurement. Connect the dots.

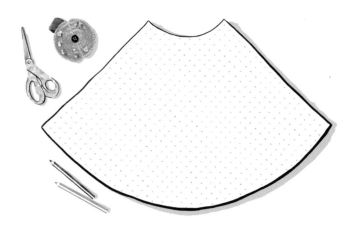

### 3. Cut pattern

Cut out your pattern using paper scissors.

### 4. Fold fabric

Fold your fabric in half lengthwise and then widthwise. You now have four layers of fabric.

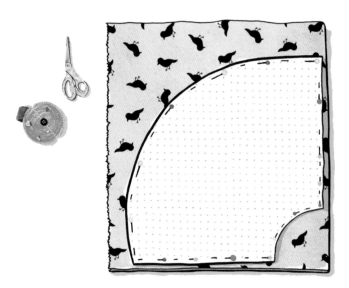

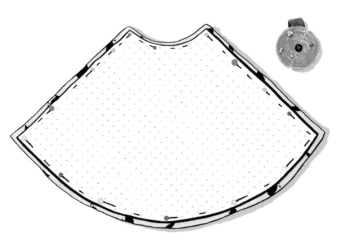

### 5. Cut fabric

Place your pattern on the fabric, lining up the edge of the pattern with the edges of the fabric. Pin around the edges. Then cut around the pattern using fabric scissors.

If your fabric is 45 inches (115 cm) wide, or if your circle is bigger than the fabric, cut two half circles and sew seams down the sides to create the same effect.

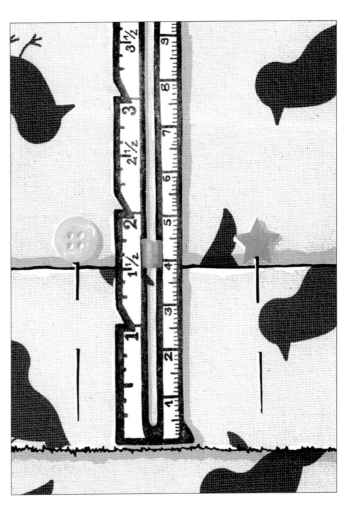

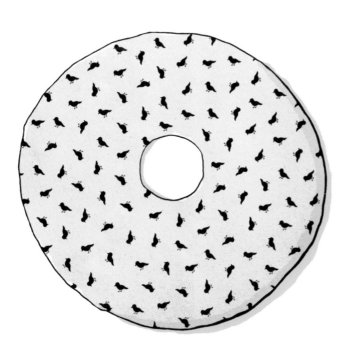

## 6. Unfold

Remove the pattern and unfold the fabric. Hello, circle!

## 7. Make waistband

Create a waistband by using your tape measure to fold
2 inches (5 cm) all the way around the top of your skirt.
Pin in place. Remove the free arm from your sewing machine
and slowly sew around, leaving a 1-inch (2.5-cm) opening.

Don't worry if your fabric
bunches up as you sew on a
curve. Once you add the elastic
it will be hardly noticeable.

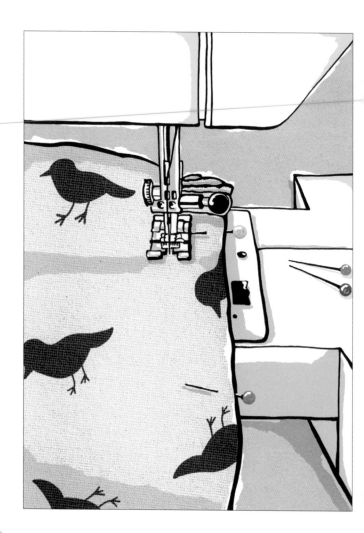

## 8. Add elastic

Cut a piece of elastic the same length as your waist
measurement. Attach a safety pin to one end of the elastic,
insert it into the waistband opening, and wiggle it around the
waistband until it comes out of the other end. Sew the ends of
the elastic together. Then sew the opening in your waistband
closed, securing the elastic in place.

## 9. Hem

Try on your skirt! Look in the mirror. If you would like a
shorter skirt, cut off some of the length. Remember that
the skirt will become ⅝ inch (1.5 cm) shorter when you
add a hem.

Create the hem by using a tape measure or ruler to help you
fold up and pin about ⅝ inch (1.5 cm) of fabric around the
bottom of the skirt. Sew the hem by machine or by hand.
Congratulations! Give it a whirl.

## How to wear your circle skirt

★ The hem should be above or a little below the knee.

★ The skirt looks cute with flat shoes or even the right pair of sneakers (sports shoes).

★ Try it high-waisted with a wide neutral-colored belt.

★ If you're feeling ambitious, make a matching skirt for your doll!

# LOVEABLE

LEGGINGS

Pattern-free, easy-to-create,
leggings to love.

Level

## What you need

- sewing basket (see page 30)
- 1–1½ yards (90–135 cm) of stretch jersey cotton fabric
- 1 yard (90 cm) of 1 inch (2.5 cm)-wide elastic
- safety pin

## — TIP —

You do not have to make a pattern for this project. But tracing the pieces, on newspaper, after you cut them out will help you make them even better next time.

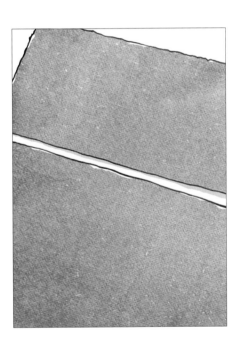

### 1. Cut fabric

Measure your waist. Use the measurement to complete this sum:

Waist measurement [      ] ÷ 2 = [      ]

Measure your fabric using the result of your sum, and then fold it in half. Cut the extra material away.

Cut down the fold creating two equal pieces. Lay one piece on top of the other, with right sides facing.

### 2. Add inseam

Fold the layered fabric in half lengthwise. Ask a friend to measure from the top of your inner leg to the bottom of your foot. This is your inseam (inside leg) measurement.

With the folded edge to the right, use chalk to mark a thin J-shape at the bottom left, measuring ¼ inch (0.5 cm) by your inseam measurement. Cut along the marked line, cutting through all four layers.

### 3. Sew a tube

Unfold the fabric and pin the layers together. Sew them together along the straight upper edges to create a tube.

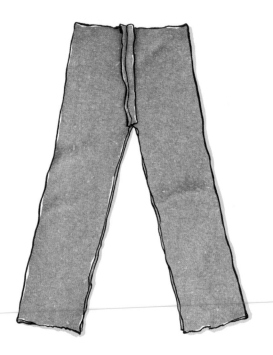

## 4. Sew the legs

Open the tube and give it a quarter turn. Line up the sewn edges (the crotch) and pin the insides of the leggings closed.

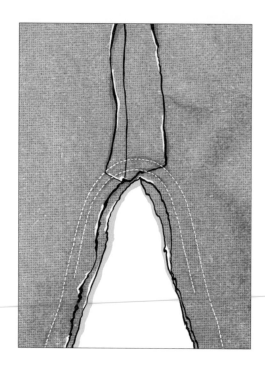

## 5. Reinforce

Sew, starting at the bottom of one leg, through the seat and down the other leg. Reinforce the seat area by adding an extra seam directly under the first one as shown in the illustration.

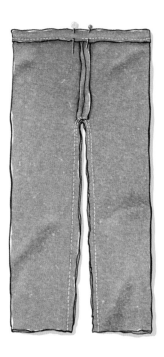

## 6. Make waistband

To make the waistband, fold over 1½ inches (4 cm) of fabric at the top. Remove your machine's extension table and sew around the waistband, leaving a small opening. Remove all the pins, except the two that mark the opening. Turn the leggings right way out.

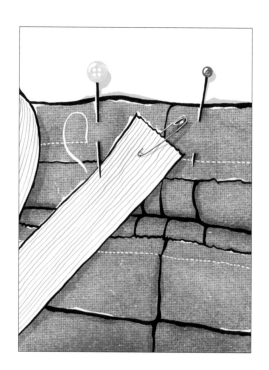

## 7. Add elastic

Cut a piece of elastic the same length as your waist measurement. Attach a safety pin to one end of the elastic, insert it into the opening, and wiggle it through the waistband until it comes out of the other end. Sew the ends of the elastic together. Sew the opening in your waistband closed, securing the elastic in place.

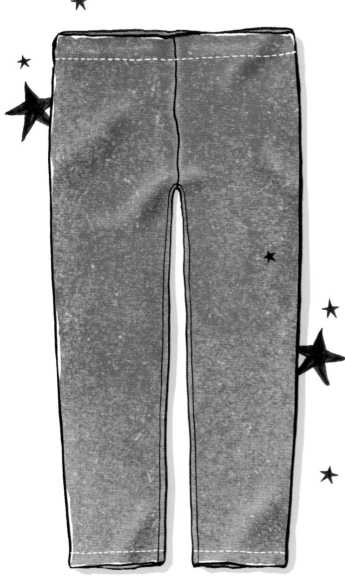

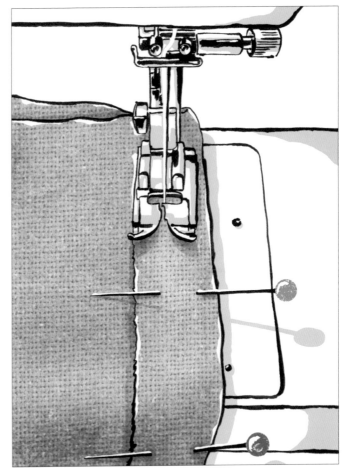

## 8. Hem

To hem the legs, use your tape measure to help you fold up and pin about ⅝ inch (1.5 cm) of fabric around the bottom of each leg. Remove the extension table from your sewing machine, and sew around each hem. Remove the pins.

Turn the leggings right side out, and they're ready to wear: Prêt-à-porter!

# LITTLE BLACK DRESS

**Say bye-bye to stress when you wear this fun-to-make dress.**

Level

## What you need

- sewing basket (see page 30)
- 1½–2 yards (135–180 cm) of cotton fabric
- 1 yard (90 cm) of 1-inch (2.5-cm) ribbon for straps (optional)
- ½ yard (45 cm) of iron-on interfacing
- 7 inches (18 cm) of zipper, snap tape (press studs), or Velcro
- newspaper or pattern paper
- calculator
- iron and ironing board
- trims (optional)

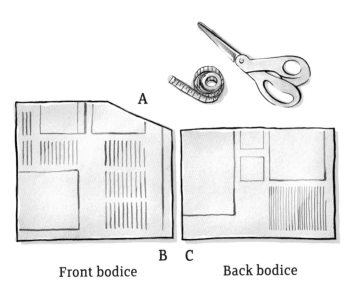

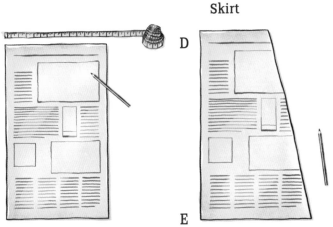

**Skirt**

Front bodice    Back bodice

## 1. Make bodice pattern

Draw your pattern! For the bodice (the top part of the dress), measure around your bust (chest) in inches and complete this sum:

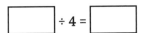 $\div 4 =$ [ ]

$+ \frac{1}{4}$ inch (0.5 cm) = [ ]

Now measure from your underarm to your high waist (the area right under your ribs). Write the measurement here:

Cut a rectangle of newspaper that is the length of the first answer multiplied by 2, and the width of the second answer. Fold one corner on a slight diagonal (A). This is the front of your bodice.

Measure and cut a piece of newspaper that is the width of the folded side (A to B) and the length of your second answer. This is the back of your bodice.

## 2. Make skirt pattern

For the skirt (the bottom part of the dress): Measure around your high waist in inches, and use the measurement to complete this sum:

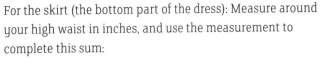 $\div 4 =$ [ ]

$+ \frac{5}{8}$ inch (1.5 cm) = [ ]

Take a piece of newspaper and use your tape measure to measure your waist answer along the top edge. Draw a mark here and then fold the paper at a slight angle as shown.

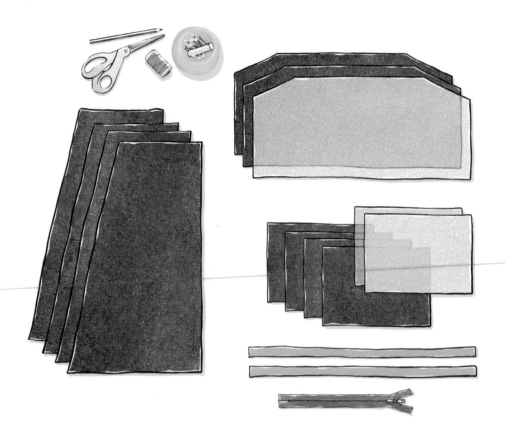

## 3. Cut fabric

Use your patterns to pin and cut the pieces of your dress.
You will need to cut:

- 2 x bodice front (one piece will be used as lining).
  Be sure to cut these on the fold of the fabric.
- 4 x bodice back (two pieces will be used as lining).
  These will be cut into individual pieces.
- 1 x bodice front in interfacing.
- 2 x bodice back in interfacing.
- 4 x skirt pieces for the front and back.

## 4. Add interfacing

Press (iron) the interfacing onto the lining of the bodice.

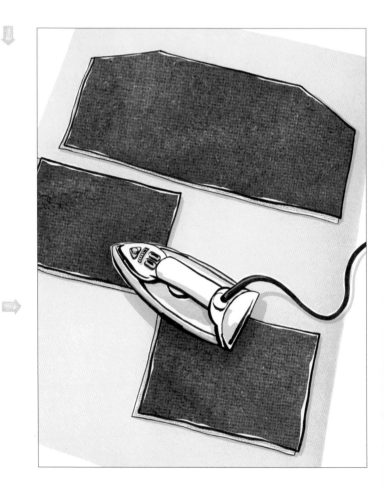

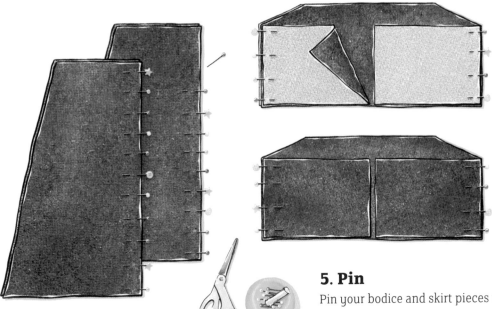

## 5. Pin

Pin your bodice and skirt pieces together as shown.

**For the bodice:** Pin the sides, right sides facing, of the bodice back and the bodice front, matching up corners B and C (shown in step 1). Repeat.

**For the skirt:** Pin two panels, matching up corners D and E. Repeat.

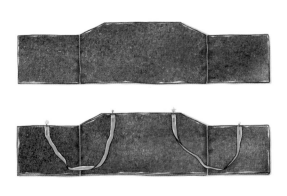

## 6. Attach straps ✋

Sew the sides of the bodice on each set. Try on the bodice and use chalk to mark the position of the straps, if you are adding them. They should be evenly spaced. Ask a friend to pin the ribbons in place for the straps while you check the fit. Cut the ribbons to the correct length and use a running stitch to hold the straps in place (this is called basting).

## 7. Sew bodice

Stack the sewn bodice panels, with right sides facing, matching up the side seams and keeping the straps hidden. Pin. Sew along the top edge.

Turn right side out, revealing the straps, and press (iron) flat.

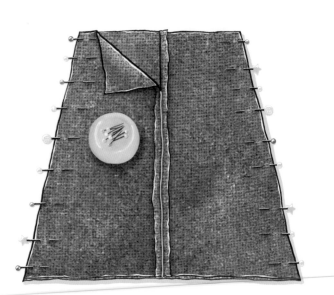

## 8. Sew skirt

Sew each set of two skirt panels together along the straight edges pinned in step 5. Leave one side open about 4 inches (10 cm) from the top. Now layer the two skirt pieces on top of each other, and pin and sew down the sides. Together, the four panels create a skirt.

## 9. Join bodice and skirt

Pin the bodice to the skirt with right sides facing. Sew around.

## 10. Add zipper

Place the zipper neatly over the bodice opening, and the opening at the top of the skirt. Pin and then hand sew the zipper in place.

It's inexpensive and quick to have a tailor at the cleaners insert the zipper for you. Alternatively, you could use Velcro or snap tape.

## 11. Hem and finish

Try your dress on and look in the mirror. Decide how long you would like the skirt to be, and trim any extra material. Next hem the skirt. Use a tape measure to help you turn under the raw edge ⅝ inch (1.5 cm) toward the skirt's wrong side. Pin and sew.

Your finished dress is a blank canvas for embellishment! Add accents such as trims, bows, or appliqué, if you like. Design your own print using fabric markers or paints.

— TIP —

The first time you make this dress, use an inexpensive fabric such as muslin (calico) to get the fit right.

# ARTSY PARTY

**You're officially Sew Fab, fashionista!**

You've earned so many fashion points that it's
time for a party in your honor. Let's celebrate you,
for being you!

Now it's time to plan your next project.
What will you do?

PAY A FASHION-FOCUSED
COMPLIMENT EACH DAY

*Display school spirit in a
Live Sparkly way*

TEACH SOMEONE
TO DO THE
RUNNING STITCH

DREAM AND SKETCH
FASHIONABLE THINGS
TO MAKE

MAKE A
RUNWAY-
WORTHY
PLAYLIST

HELP A FRIEND
DISCOVER HER

STYLE TRIBE

CREATE COSTUMES
FOR A PLAY

 SAVE SCRAPS AND SEW
SCARVES FOR GIFTS

WRITE YOUR
OWN FASHION
HOW-TO

SEW A BACKDROP
OUT OF OLD CLOTHES

# DESIGN A RUNWAY WITH RIBBONS

HAVE A FASHION SHOW
WITH FRIENDS

BECOME A FASHION
REPORTER

*Set monthly dates to
craft junky jewels*

SPREAD
THE WORD
ABOUT

**START A FASHION BLOG**

 SHARE YOUR SMILE

DIY

 WEAR ART

# NEVER STOP CREATING

 LEARN TO TAKE FASHION PHOTOS

MAKE A BOW AND ATTACH
A CHEERFUL NOTE

Set up a photo shoot

MAKE OUTFITS
FOR PETS

# LAUNCH A ZINE

 *give something
you make away*

# Glossary

**Accessory:**
item such as a hair clip, piece of jewelry, purse, or scarf that can be worn or carried to complete an outfit

**Appliqué:**
a small piece of fabric attached by hand or machine to a larger piece of fabric to create a design

**Basting (Tacking) Stitch:**
a loose stitch used to hold fabric in place temporarily

**Bobbin:**
a small plastic or metal spool that fits under your sewing machine needle plate and holds thread

**Casing:**
a folded and stitched tube to hold elastic or cord

**Chic:**
stylish

**Contrast:**
the state of being different

**Details:**
the separate parts of a look as they relate to the whole, from head to toe

**DIY:**
stands for "Do It Yourself"

**Embellish:**
to decorate with appliqué, trim, or notions

**Eyewear:**
fashionable glasses or sunglasses

**Fabric:**
a woven or knit material made from fibers

**Fashion:**
expression of beauty through clothes

**Faux:**
French word for fake

**Go-to Accessory:**
an accessory that always looks great on you

**Grainline:**
a long arrow printed on a pattern that corresponds to the lengthwise direction of the fabric

**Hem:**
the finished edge at the bottom of a garment or sleeve

**Hue:**
color or shade

**Individuality:**
the state of being yourself (and not a trendy robot)

**Inspiration:**
the urge to do something creative

**Jewelry:**
accessories, such as bracelets, necklaces, or rings. Jewelry can be made of precious metals or set with real or faux gems

**Lining:**
a second layer of fabric that covers the inside of a garment or accessory

**Live Sparkly:**
a Sew Fab idea, meaning to wear accessories that add flashes of fun to your fashion

**Machine Needle:**
a small, very thin, needle that is used in a sewing machine

**Must-have:**
wearable fashion to keep in your closet (wardrobe) from season to season

**Neutral:**
Having a color that does not attract attention. Examples are black, white, and browns

**Notions (Haberdashery):**
objects attached to a garment for decorative purposes, or to serve a function, such as zippers, buttons, and snaps

**Organize:**
to arrange or order things so that they can be found or used easily and quickly

**Pattern:**
paper in the shape of the parts of a garment or accessory

**Pin:**
thin, straight piece of metal used to fasten things together

**Pincushion:**
a pillow used to store pins and needles

**Pinking Shears:**
fabric scissors that leave a zigzag pattern instead of a straight edge. The zigzag pattern prevents the edges from fraying

**Point Turner:**
a small tool, such as a pencil or chopstick, that can be used to get inside a tight corner or small space for ease of pressing

**Print:**
a textile or garment with a colored design or pattern

**Quality:**
a degree of excellence

**Raw Edge:**
the unfinished cut end of a piece of fabric

**Right Side:**
the side of the fabric that is seen when the garment is worn

**Seam:**
the joining of two or more fabrics with thread to make stitches

**Seam Ripper:**
a tool used for unpicking stitches

**Sharps:**
needles that are used for hand sewing

**Silhouette:**
shape or outline of someone or something

**Statement Piece:**
bold accessory that may be a little
outside the wearer's comfort zone

**Style:**
how you piece together your look
using fashion

**Style Tribe:**
your fashion family (see page 8)

**Stylist:**
a person who creates and maintains
a certain style

**Tape Measure:**
a strip of flexible plastic used to
measure fabric and take body
measurements

**Thread:**
a fine cord of fibers, such as cotton
or polyester

**Trend:**
what's in fashion right now, and what's
next in fashion

**Trim:**
materials like ribbons, lace, and
sequins, which can be neatly sewn
on to a garment

**Wardrobe:**
a collection of clothes

**Wrong Side:**
the side of the fabric that should not be
seen (the opposite of the Right Side)

**Zigzag:**
a machine stitch that goes from right
to left and looks like a long string of
zzzzzzzzzzzs

## About the author

Lesley Ware is a teaching artist, style blogger, and designer living in Brooklyn, New York. In 2008, she started a blog, thecreativecookie.com, which quickly became a destination for a behind-the-scenes look at fashion in New York City. Lesley runs popular sewing and crafting workshops for girls and hopes that this book will encourage them to use fashion as a creative outlet of expression, and thus give fashion a more interesting future.

## Many thanks to...

My fashion students for their constant inspiration and feedback while writing this book. I'm fortunate to be surrounded by oodles of super-smart fashionistas.

Sabine Pieper for her lovely illustrations. It's been a dream to have my words with such whimsical art.

The wonderful folks at Laurence King for publishing this book and making it ummmm Sew Fab! Especially Helen Rochester, Sarah Batten, and Clare Double with whom I've had the pleasure of working the most.

The designer, Eleanor Ridsdale, for bringing your creativity and keen detail to these pages.

Andrea Somberg, my agent, for moving the process along swiftly and helping me understand as we go.

The warm circle of ladies who were my sounding board as I shaped ideas for "find your style tribe," you know who you are.

kamau ware, my very talented husband, for believing in me always. It's been wonderful to have you in my corner – what a lucky cookie I am!

My parents, Gwen and Herbert, for encouraging my artsy style and creativity. Endless gratitude to my mom for being brave enough to teach a four-year-old how to sew.

The girls reading this book. Sew Fab is a feeling that you'll have once you are able to define your style and make your own clothes. If you can speak up with fashion you can in other ways too. Be different, be better, be legendary, be YOU!